Fixey Fox Lights the Night

Copyright © 2023 by JeffrAy N. Kessler
All world rights reserved

Illustrations by Susan Kessler and Tajin Robles

This is a work of fiction. Names, places, and incidents are the products of the author's imagination or are used fictitiously. Any resemblance to actual events or locales or persons, living or dead, is entirely coincidental.

No part of this book may be reproduced, stored in a retrieval system, or transmitted in any form or by any means electronic, mechanical, photocopying, recording or otherwise, without the prior consent of the publisher.

Readers are encouraged to go to www.MissionPointPress.com to contact the author or to find information on how to buy this book in bulk at a discounted rate.

Published by Mission Point Press
2554 Chandler Rd.
Traverse City, MI 49696
(231) 421-9513
www.MissionPointPress.com

Book design by Sarah Meiers

ISBN 978-1-958363-97-3
Library of Congress Control Number XXXX

Printed in the United States of America

Fixey Fox
Lights
The Night

Jeffray N. Kessler

Illustrations by Susan Kessler and Tajin Robles

MISSION POINT PRESS

This book is dedicated to the people who work at gardens and farms, and to the teachers and parents who help children to learn and grow.

Snap...Snap...Snap. The sound made one of the young sleeping fox's ears shoot straight up. And then, *Snap, Snap, Snap,* the sound became louder and quicker. The snaps made the fox's heart go pitter-pat, and then both silky, furry ears were standing up high and facing forward. The fox's eyes blinked awake, and opened wide. He knew he was being warned of danger by his friend, the farmer's son. The snap was a signal that the fox's keen ears could hear even from far away. The boy snapped the alert by using his finger and thumb.

This time the boy snapped faster and faster, and the fox saw why as he looked out from his hiding place. He was tucked behind a bale of straw in a wagon parked just outside of the barn.

He saw the farmer walking directly to the wagon. She held a rope that was attached to his very large friend, Admiral Walker. Walking behind this bull was the boy. He was trying to warn the fox that the farmer and the bull were coming.

The fox got the message, and could see that the farmer planned to lead the bull into the wagon, but there was no escape. He was not worried about Admiral Walker. They were friends, but he did not want the farmer to see him. He did not trust her. Most farmers do not trust foxes either. It was too late to run, so the fox sank down deeper into the straw. His red-orange fur was covered by straw and shadows.

The bull suddenly stopped, and refused to move forward, even though the farmer tugged as hard as she could on the rope. The boy caught up, and hugged the large animal. The bull was very special to the boy. He had raised it from the time it was a newborn calf.

"Come on, you big ox!" shouted the farmer. The large animal rocked its head back and forth.

The boy knew that his bull did not like to be called an ox. "Mom, his name is 'Admiral Walker,' and he is a bull, not an ox."

"Well then, all right," said his mother, the farmer. She turned to the bull, gave a gentler tug, and said, "Please, *bull* Admiral Walker, get into the trailer. We are going to take a ride."

The boy whispered in the bull's ear, "Everything will be fine. I promise."

With that, Admiral Walker, the boy's special pet, the bull that had won all the prizes at the county fair, slowly stepped forward into the wagon.

The farmer walked around to the front of the wagon and hooked it to a team of strong workhorses while the boy latched the back gate of the wagon in place. The fox could see the sadness in the boy's face. He heard the farmer say, "I need you to stay here and take care of the other animals. I know it is hard to say good-bye to Admiral Walker. I am very proud of you for how you raised this champion bull, but now it is time to sell him, and our farm could really use the money. I will be back soon."

The farmer hugged her son, and climbed up onto the wagon seat. She called for her horses to "giddyap," and they pulled ahead. The wagon jerked forward, causing Admiral Walker to lose his balance.

He accidentally stepped into the corner where the fox was hiding. "Hey, you big ox. You stepped on my toe!" the fox said. "Now I cannot jump out of the wagon."

Admiral Walker looked down and said, "I'm a bull, not an ox, and I am sorry I stepped on your toe." It was at that moment that both Admiral Walker and the fox heard a '*Snap!*' They both looked back to see the boy waving, and wiping tears from

his eyes. They knew they were the boy's closest friends. What they did not know was where they were going, but somehow, they believed they would see the boy again.

The bumpy ride started out very slowly. The wheels squeaked and rocked the wagon from side to side. Admiral Walker and his friend the fox could hear the farmer singing up front, and talking to her horses. It was a beautiful, late fall day. The air was clear and cool, and filled with the smells of nearby farms. Hay was being mowed, crops were being harvested, and dirt was being turned. After several hours and through the night, all those smells seemed to go away.

The fox said, "I think we are now far away from home."

Admiral Walker replied, "We are seeing new sights and hearing new sounds. Where do you think we are going?" As clever as the fox was, he could not answer that question. Admiral Walker said, "I just hope it is another nice farm."

As more time passed, a new smell filled the air. It was a sweet mixture of animals and flowers. It caused the fox and Admiral Walker to look out over the edge of the wagon. They were surprised by what they saw.

The farmer slowed the trailer to a stop. She also seemed surprised as she looked around. There were two huge barns, and garages filled with carriages. Fields of vegetables spread out in many directions. A variety of animals grazed in pastures covered with lush green grasses. Amongst it all were blanket after blanket after blanket of colorful flowers. It looked as if a rainbow had come down from the sky to lie on the ground. This farm was surrounded in part by a forest that seemed to sing as the wind gently caused limbs and leaves of many colors to dance and sway.

With great excitement, the fox turned to Admiral Walker and said, "Look at those beautiful woods! I can hide there. I can dig a new burrow. I can live there and be safe."

Admiral Walker replied, "I am happy for you, fox, but I am seeing fields of green grass and two sturdy barns that I think I am going to like."

From her seat at the front of the wagon, the farmer stood up. The fox slid back into his hiding place behind the straw while she admired the crops, grazing animals, people working together, strong barns, and seemingly endless woodlands that climbed up the hill behind. As she turned back to the front, the fox decided this would be a good time to escape. He checked his injured toe, and it seemed much better. He whispered to Admiral Walker, "I will come and see you later, but for now, I must head to the safety of the woods."

The big bull replied, "Good luck, my clever, furry friend."

The fox scampered out of the wagon, and scurried quickly to the edge of the forest. He stopped for a moment to look back. He was happy to see the farmer driving her wagon toward one of the barns where other cattle were grazing.

Deeper into the woods the fox ran, darting over roots, around stumps, behind trees, and through brush. He was surprised to see tiny houses here and there as he explored this new wooded wonderland. Even though he wanted to know more about the little houses, he started to realize that he was quite tired, having not slept at all during the trip. It was not long before he came upon a very thick tangle of branches. It looked like a perfect, safe place to hide and take a nap. He nestled down below the woodsy curtain, curled his tail around, and was soon sound asleep.

A sunset filled with bright streaks of color soon welcomed the dark of night and a sky sprinkled with twinkles. The fox was still enjoying his deep sleep when soft, silly voices caused one of his ears to perk up straight, just like when his friend the boy made his snapping sound. The voices giggled quietly, and caused the fox's other ear to perk right up as well. The little voices seemed to be coming from all sides of him. Sure enough, as he opened his eyes and peered around, he realized they were coming from everywhere. He was surrounded, but by what or whom?

The fox sat up. He felt lucky that he could see so well in the dark, because he was having a hard time believing what he was seeing. Even though he had lived his whole life in the woodlands, he had never seen so many. A big smile spread across his face, and he said, "You are fairies and gnomes. I love fairies and gnomes!"

With that, the band of miniature characters began clapping their hands, and started singing and dancing in a circle around the fox. Some had wings. Many wore artful hats and colorful jackets. He noticed their shoes had toes that curled up. Their ears reminded him of his own because they were big too, and stood straight up. He could not take his eyes off their eyes because they seemed to glow with gentleness and alertness. How talented they were. They had sweet voices, they leapt, twirled, and danced, and some played tiny musical instruments.

Soon the singing and dancing paused, and the circle of fairies moved in closer. They had many questions for the fox, and he had many for them. They learned about each other. The fox told his story of arriving in the wagon, and the fairies explained that they lived there in their little homes as part of the farm. This was a very special farm. It

had animals and crops but it was also adorned with many flower gardens, trees and sculptures. It was called a botanic garden.

They all decided to be friends, and the fairies took the fox on a parade around the woods to show off their houses. It was a parade of homes.

The fairies were very proud. They kept giggling as they walked along, because the fox was so much bigger than they were. They showed him how they used many materials from the woods for their houses: sticks, stones, leaves, mushrooms, flowers, bark, and many other things that made each one very special. It was clear to the fox that the fairies, as builders, were filled with art and joy, but he also noticed something else. Some of the houses had broken parts. Several times the parade would stop while the fox offered to fix a broken twig with a stronger stick or move a larger stone in place of a small one. Since he was bigger, he could do these things much easier than his new friends could.

The gnomes and fairies thanked the fox and were glad to have a new neighbor. In fact, as the parade came to an end, one of the gnomes said in a small, squeaky voice, "I think we should call you 'Fixey' because you fixed so many things for us today." The rest of the fairies agreed, and began to chant, "Fixey, Fixey, Fixey."

The fox, now "Fixey," was so happy to be part of this woods. "What a perfect spot for my new home," he thought. He was troubled by one thing. He wondered why or how so many of the little fairy houses had become damaged. When he asked that question, all the fairies turned to him and became quiet. Two of them came forward and told Fixey about a group of six animals in the woods, called coyotes, that were not very nice.

"Their fur is usually rumpled and dirty, and

they have gleaming white eyes that shine at night. Although not all coyotes are bad, this bunch seems to like to scare us, the farmers, and the other animals on the farm. Sometimes they run by our houses and step on them with their big paws on purpose. Nobody at the farm likes these coyotes, but they cannot seem to catch them."

Fixey listened, and said, "I'll just have to see if I can fix that." He did not tell them that he had experience with coyotes on his other farm. He knew these animals very well.

The sun was just starting to come up over the farm. The sky glowed as it peeked through the trees. The fairies knew it was time for them to go back into their houses, and Fixey was ready for some rest too. It had been a long, fun, and interesting night. As he curled up in his cozy lair, he smiled at his new name. "I am now 'Fixey,'" he thought. "I like it."

In the next days, Fixey and the fairies became

very good friends and neighbors. They worked together to fix many fairy houses. This was important, because soon it would be winter. The temperatures were already getting cooler.

One day, Fixey came up with a plan to fix the coyote problem by keeping them away. "We will make a signal system," he said. "I have very good hearing, and I know you do too. Can you snap your fingers?"

The fairies all nodded. The plan was to have fairies hidden in the woods at night as watching and listening guards. "When any of you guards hear the coyotes coming down through the woods, begin snapping your fingers. I will hear your snapping, and when the coyotes get close, I will scream so loudly that they will run away in fear. Luckily, screaming is one of the many sounds we foxes can make."

It did not take long for their plan to be tested.

In fact, that very night, Fixey heard the guard fairies and gnomes snapping their fingers. The coyotes were headed toward them through the dark woods. Fixey quickly stood tall on his back legs and waited. He could hear them crashing through the brush, and then he saw twelve icy white eyes charging toward the fairy village. It was time for action, and with all his voice, Fixey let out his loudest fox scream. It was a piercing shriek that scared the coyotes so much that they quickly turned, and ran back the way they had come. Fixey doubted they would ever come back to that part of the woods again.

    The fairies and gnomes were shocked and very happy, and now felt that they could sleep better at night. Their homes were safe. They began to take turns being guards. Fixey was happy that the plan worked, and he wondered what he might discover next on this new farm. He also wondered how his friend Admiral Walker was doing.

The next day, several fairies took Fixey for a walk to see the farm and to meet and make new friends. It was important for the fairies to be along on this walk, because a fox, by himself, that nobody knew would not be welcome on the farm. Other animals often thought of foxes as being scary. The fairies and Fixey wanted to prove them wrong.

The day was cool. It felt like winter was getting closer when the fairies and Fixey came out of the woods. The fairies reminded him that this farm was called the Botanic Garden. Again, Fixey was amazed at its size and all the activity that was going on.

Their first stop was at something called the labyrinth. It looked like a grand porch with what appeared to be a map of lines made of bricks. A family of deer stood nearby. At first, they turned to run when they saw Fixey, but the fairies waved and whistled. That got the deer's attention, and they wondered what the fairies were excited about. The fairies introduced Fixey, and explained that they need not worry, because he was a new friend and he was a fixer. The deer took turns telling Fixey about their jobs.

The mother deer said, "We are wild animals, so we do not really live on the farm. We live close to the farm, and very near this labyrinth. It is a peaceful place."

The father deer added, "We spend much of our time right here, welcoming all living creatures and people to the labyrinth."

A young deer then stepped forward to say, "The farmers give us corn and other treats for our help."

Fixey nodded and said, "It must be just wonderful to have this relationship with the farm. It seems perfect."

The deer agreed, but the father deer did say, "If

there were no coyotes, it would be perfect. Maybe you can fix that."

"I will think about it," replied Fixey. "I hope to see you again soon."

Fixey turned to the fairies and asked, "Where to next?"

"Right this way," said the fairies. Soon they came upon what looked like a big stone fence. The fairies explained that it was the lower floor of what used to be a barn for horses. It was filled with flowers, and of course there was a horse nearby. Just like the deer, the horse was worried to see a fox, but the fairies explained that Fixey was a friend, and the horse calmed down.

"Welcome to the Botanic Garden and farm," said the horse. "At first, I thought you were one of those coyotes. Watch out for them."

Fixey said, "I will be very careful. I am glad to meet you. I hope to fix that coyote problem."

Next, the fairies invited Fixey into the horse-barn garden, inside the walls. They told him that it was called the "wall garden." It was warmer there inside the walls, and the flowers must have loved it, because they were very beautiful. Bees still buzzed around from blossom to blossom. Fixey was enjoying the sights, but he thought he heard some growling sounds nearby, maybe even a little roar.

"Do you fairies hear that?" asked Fixey.

The fairies laughed and said, "It wasn't us, but walk around the corner into the 'secret garden,' and you will see."

Fixey did just that, and sure enough, there were two grey lions, sitting very still. One had a ball in its mouth. Before he could even ask, the lions introduced themselves. They said, "We are lions, and as long as we have this ball, it is our job to protect this garden world. We can growl and roar, but because we are stone, we cannot chase."

"Well, lions, I am quite good at chasing. Foxes are very fast. Maybe I can help you." The fairies told the lions more about Fixey, and Fixey said he would come back.

"Great," said the lions. "Because even our friend, the slowpoke turtle, is faster than us."

"Hey, I heard that, you lions!" said a soft but clear voice.

It was not the lions talking. Fixey was not sure where the voice came from, but the fairies knew. They pointed just below the fence. Fixey peeked under, and found himself staring right into the face of a turtle.

"Yep. It was me," said the turtle. "Are you our new friend?"

"Yep. That's me," said Fixey. "Nice to meet you."

"Same to you," said the turtle. "Come on out of there. Let's talk."

Fixey first turned to the lions and gave them a wave, and then he and the fairies ran quickly out of the walled garden. They found the turtle walking slowly around the wagon garages, so they followed along. They all came to a very special garden with a big statue of a cow and a babbling brook. "This is where I like to be," said the turtle. "You are always welcome here."

Fixey said, "It seems like a very calm place. I was going to ask you if it was your home, but it looks like you carry your house on your back. Not like the fairies."

"That is true," said the turtle. "But you know what I wish I had? Your speed. I hear foxes are very fast. Not like us turtles."

Fixey replied, "Hmmm. Now there is a tough problem to fix, but you know what? Maybe your slowness is not a problem at all. Speed isn't everything. Instead of thinking of yourself as slow, you

should think of yourself as careful. How do you feel about that?"

"What I think is, I like you, Fixey. You fixed my problem by proving it is not a problem at all," said the turtle, with a big smile on his face.

Right about then, Fixey looked up from his quiet spot next to the brook, and was happy to see his friend Admiral Walker across the field, looking in one of the barn windows. He asked the fairies, "Can we walk over to see my friend?" Fixey pointed, and the fairies were a bit surprised.

They asked, "Is that big ox your friend?"

"Be careful now, my fairy chums. His name is Admiral Walker, and he does not like to be called on ox. He is a bull. Come on, it is my turn to introduce you."

Fixey shouted, "Hey, big guy!"

Admiral Walker turned slowly, and was very

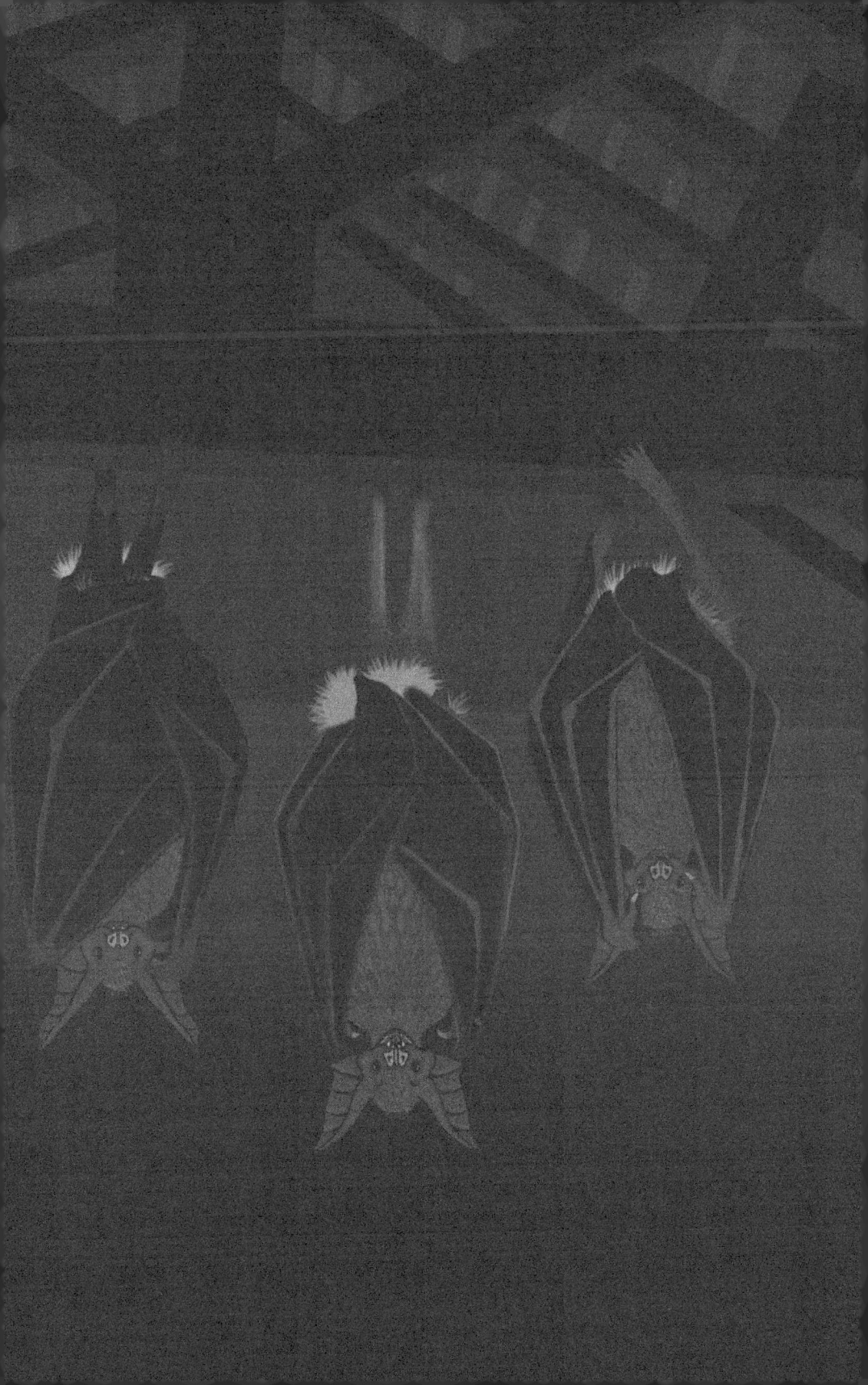

happy to see his fox friend. Fixey said, "These are my new pals, the fairies."

The fairies all smiled, waved, and said, "You are the biggest *bull* we have ever seen."

Admiral Walker nodded at the fairies, and then looked back at Fixey. He said, "I too have a new friend. Look in the window, and say hi to Colantha the cow. We have been talking about having a baby."

Colantha looked up and said, "Hello. Admiral Walker has told me much about you and how clever you are. I hope you come by to visit very often. By the way, would you like to meet three bats that hang out here in the barn with me and the other cows? Their names are Biff, Bop, and Bart. You will like them, I think."

Fixey and the fairies went into the barn to say hi to the bats, but it was daytime, so they were all asleep. They agreed to come back later. They all waved good-bye to Admiral Walker and Colantha,

and the fairies led Fixey behind the barn. There they came upon a large gathering of butterflies in what the fairies called the pollinator garden. There were bees too. Since it was getting colder each day, there were not too many flowers left. Seeing that, the fairies asked the butterflies what was going on. It turned out that the butterflies were getting ready to leave for a warmer place to live during the winter.

The fairies said, "We are glad we caught you before you left, because we want to introduce you to our new friend, Fixey the fox. He will be here this winter and next spring when you return. He likes to fix things."

The butterflies waved and fluttered their wings, and one monarch named Sara said, "Maybe Fixey can keep those coyotes out of these flower beds. They stomp all over the plants."

Fixey said, "I will see what I can do, but for

now I want to wish you a safe trip. I will see your children in the spring."

Although Fixey did not know it, all day long he was being watched by a golden hawk and her two crow pals. The fairies pointed them out high above a very special garden. "This garden is called 'Fire Wise,'" they said. "These birds are like the deer in some ways. They are wild, so they don't live on the farm, but near it. Their job is to watch for smoke or fire from up there. They make the whole farm safer. The farmers bring them treats too."

Fixey waved his bright orange, bushy tail at the birds, and they flapped their wings back. He said, "I hope to meet them up close some time soon."

Fixey and the fairies realized they had put in a very full day. They were tired. The sun was setting, surrounded by heavy gray clouds, and the air was getting cooler and cooler. They all headed back to the woods for some rest. While the fairies went to

their little houses, other fairies came out into the early night to listen for the coyotes. They would be ready to snap their fingers as a warning and alert Fixey. Fixey returned to his burrow. He rested, but his ears were up.

When morning came, even though the sun rose strong and bright, there was a surprise for Fixey and his friends in the woods. The ground and branches were coated with a light frost. The sun's rays made the crystals light up, as if everything was covered with a blanket of diamonds. Winter seemed closer than Fixey and the fairies thought.

It was a restful night's sleep for Fixey. There were no alarms. Maybe the coyotes learned a lesson about coming to this part of the woods. The quiet start to the morning gave Fixey a chance to think a little. The day before, he had met many new friends at the Botanic Garden and farm. Some had problems that he would try to fix. First, he had an idea for the deer that lived by the labyrinth. He decided to go see them first. The fairies still seemed to be sleeping, so he walked out of the woods by himself.

The deer were grazing in the grass near the labyrinth. Fixey noticed that the labyrinth was coated with frost, but with the sun rising higher, he did not think it would last very long. He wished the deer good morning, and said, "I have an idea that might help you with the coyote problem. In the woods, when the coyotes are near, the fairies snap their fingers as an alarm. I hear those snaps because of my good hearing. I then use one of my many voices to make a loud, screeching scream. It causes the coyotes to run away. I know you can't snap because you don't have any fingers, but what if you stomped a hoof on the labyrinth's hard bricks?"

The deer tried this, and the sound was very close to the snap of a fairy's fingers. The deer smiled and thought this just might work, so they agreed to take turns staying up a little later at night to listen for the coyotes.

"Don't you worry now," said Fixey. "You listen. You stomp. I'll hear, and I'll scream. We'll see if we can scare those coyotes away."

Fixey said good-bye to the deer, and as he turned toward the farm, he noticed there were many workers taking care of the animals, the crops, and the flowers at the large farm. This worried Fixey, because he knew that most people did not trust foxes, especially on a farm. He thought it would be best to stay out of sight for now.

Luckily, he spied Admiral Walker across the field, again looking into the same barn window. He decided he would wish him and Colantha a good morning. He darted behind the barn, took a moment to look up at the golden hawk and the two crows, and wave. The birds nodded and kept watch. Fixey then slipped around the barn and got between

Admiral Walker and the wall. He said, "Good morning, Admiral. Did you have a good night's rest? How is Colantha?"

"I slept well," said Admiral Walker.

"And so did I," said Colantha, on the other side of the window.

Just as they were about to have a nice chat, Fixey noticed two farmers coming toward them. To be safe, he jumped up through Colantha's window to hide. He heard the farmers talking about Admiral Walker and Colantha. They were hoping Colantha would have many babies. They left food for both of them, and walked away.

Fixey munched some of the food, and the three friends talked about what a wonderful farm this was, sharing what each liked best about the botanic-garden farm. Colantha offered to walk with Fixey to the other end of the barn to see if the bats, Biff, Bop, and Bart, might be awake.

Only Admiral Walker noticed a familiar wagon coming up the road to the farm. He looked closely, and was happy to see it was the same wagon he and Fixey had ridden in, and it was being driven by the young boy, his best friend, and his mother the farmer. They were bringing more animals to the farm: pigs and sheep. The wagon was covered with a rope net so they would not jump out.

The wagon stopped, and in just a moment, the boy stood up and saw Admiral Walker. He raced across the field and jumped up to hug the huge pet. It was a reunion with tears and laughter. The boy shared stories about what had been happening. The boy said that he and his mother might just stay here at this farm and work. The bull nodded his great head.

After a bit, the boy asked about the fox. "Have you seen him?" With his big, soft nose, Admiral Walker nudged the boy's hand. The boy asked,

"What are you doing?" Admiral Walker nudged his hand again, and this time the boy got the message. He stood back, held his hand in the air, and snapped his fingers.

Inside the barn, Fixey had been getting to know Biff, Bop, and Bart, but when he heard that snap, he stopped and listened. There it was again, and Fixey knew exactly where it had come from. He ran out of the barn, saw the boy, and leapt into his arms. He wrapped his soft tail around the boy's neck. The boy stroked Fixey's head, and the two could not have been happier to be reunited. They were back together again.

There was so much to explain that Fixey jumped down and led the boy into the woods to meet the fairies. The fairies could tell the boy what had been happening. Once in the woods, Fixey called out to the fairies with a soft song. They came out, but were startled to see the boy. Fixey made a circle around the fairies to assure them all was safe. The boy sat down, and the fairies told him about the farm, their little houses in the woods, the coyotes, and how Fixey had been able to help many new friends. One fairy said, "Oh, yes. By the way, the fox's name is now 'Fixey,' because he fixes so many things. He lives here in the woods with us."

The boy was quite amazed to be seeing and hearing so many fairies. He then let them know that he wanted to be their friend, and there was nothing to fear from him. He said he and Fixey had lived on another farm together, along with that big bull, Admiral Walker. "My mother is a farmer," he said. "She brought us back here with more animals, hoping that we would be asked to stay and work."

The boy continued, "Now I heard you mention coyotes. I want to learn more about them, because on our other farm, Fixey and I came up with a plan that got rid of our coyotes once and for all. Just

maybe this plan will work here. I will have to talk to some of the other people and see what I can learn and share."

The boy then thought it was best to go back to his mother and help her. He also wanted to meet some of the people and talk about the coyotes. Most of all, he wanted to tell his mother how much he would like to stay there.

Fixey and the fairies remained in the woods for the time being. The fairies were excited after meeting the boy and learning that he and Fixey might be able to get rid of the coyotes for good, but it was daytime, and that was when fairies slept. They headed back into their houses and Fixey went to his burrow.

After another quiet, cool night, Fixey was surprised to see a little snow on the ground in the morning. He stretched and stood up, breathing in the crisp air. He decided he would check on the deer, the horse, the lions, and the turtle before all the people came out to do their work. He ran from place to place very fast, stretching out his legs and stirring up the snow. He noticed little sparkling crystals of ice that gathered on his tail. Running fast felt very good. He had almost forgotten that it was one of his favorite things.

When he returned to the woods, the boy was waiting for him by his burrow. He explained that in a little while there was going to be a meeting of all the workers on the farm. He thought this would be a perfect time to introduce Fixey, and assure the people that he would do no harm, but instead could help them.

"Fixey, I want to share with them how we got rid of the coyotes, using our net and your fast running in the snow, just like your great-great-grandfather did. Would you be willing to do this?" Fixey nodded. The two of them walked out of the woods toward one of the barns where the meeting was to be.

When the boy and Fixey walked into the barn, everyone jumped back in shock. The boy and even his mother were quick to explain that this fox was very special, not like the foxes they knew. He was here to help. Soon the workers began talking about the coyotes. "We can't catch them, because they come only in the night. They can see so well in the dark, and they seem to know we cannot. They can see us and the animals, but we cannot see them."

The boy spoke up. "At our other farm, we had coyotes, and we were able to get rid of them because of this fox. You see, he is a Fire Fox. The legend of the Fire Fox lives in him. His father, grandfather, and great-grandfather were also Fire Foxes. A Fire Fox can turn a night sky into a bright sky. They do this by running very fast, and dragging their bushy tails across the snow. Crystals of snow shoot into the sky from their tails, filling it with bright light. You will have to see it to believe it. On our farm, the light surprised the coyotes, and gave us a better chance. We could never catch coyotes in the dark, but with the sky made bright by this fox running through the snow, we finally caught them. We could see them as well as they could see us. Your farm is much bigger than ours was. There are more coyotes here, so you will have to be spread out and be ready with nets for just the right moment to capture the shocked coyotes. Even though there are six of them, there are many more of us, and we will be able to see them. I think this can work if you are willing to try."

The workers all agreed to give the amazing plan a chance. They had nets from other tries hanging in the loft of the second barn. All they needed was more snow, and the next day, they got their wish. They woke to a fresh blanket of snow. It fell softly the night before, and the morning was still and quiet. Fixey saw the perfect snow conditions, and he knew it was time for him to gather his new friends: the fairies, the deer, the horse, the turtle, the bats, the hawk, the crows, and Admiral Walker to explain the plan, and how they could help. They met in the walled garden by the lions, since they could not move.

Fixey said, "Tonight we are going to catch all six coyotes. We must surprise them with the noises you make, and the bright sky and screams I can make. Lions, I know you can roar. Fairies, I have heard you snap your fingers all at once and shout. Deer, I know you can bray and stomp. Horse, you do the same. Bats, I want you to dive and screech. Admiral Walker, I want you to get as many of the livestock as you can to moo and moan louder than you ever have before. Hawk and crows, you are to listen for the signal from your perch, and then caw

and shriek. This will alert all of us to begin making noise. You must be loud. For that first signal, we need you, turtle. In a little while, the boy will come and get you, and put you in our wagon along with two fairies. He will pull the wagon in front of the first barn. The fairies will have sticks, and when they see me start to run, they will drum on your back. That is the signal. You then take it from there, hawk and crows. Have you all got your jobs? Do you believe we can do this?"

The team of animals and fairies shouted, "Yes, we can!"

With the animals ready, snow on the ground, the people spread out around the fields, holding their nets. Fixey was ready too. All they could do was wait for night to come. Darkness came with silence at first. It was so quiet that Fixey could almost feel it.

At first, the sheep and goats started to stir.

They knew danger was near. The coyotes were coming. Fixey began to run. The fairies saw Fixey, and drummed on the turtle's back. The golden hawk and the crows shouted their alert, and animal sounds came from all directions: roars, shrieks, moos, moans, squeaks, and brays. The bats and birds took to the sky, ready to dive.

And Fixey ran faster and faster around the fences of the fields and gardens. He ran so fast that his tail whisked ice crystals from the top of the snow into the sky, where they became glassy streaks of bright light and color. Indeed, the night sky became a bright sky, just as the boy had said it would.

The noises and the bright sky confused the coyotes. They were stunned into stillness, and that was long enough for the workers and farmers to capture them with their nets: all six. They could see them!

Fixey kept running until the coyotes were

placed in wagons with the nets still around them. The coyotes struggled against the nets, but this only made them tighter. Workers quickly drove their wagons away. The coyotes would be taken to a forest many miles from the farm, never to trouble any farm again.

As the last wagon left, Fixey stopped running. In fact, he ran into the arms of the boy, very tired. The boy could feel Fixey's heart beating fast, and his bushy tail was still filled with sparkling ice crystals. He carried Fixey to the walled garden where the animals and fairies had gathered. There was cheering and singing and relief. Life on the farm had just gotten better with the coyotes gone. They had all helped. They all had a job to do, and they did it. Soon the workers and farmers joined the celebration. As the sky began to slowly dim, a gentle snow began to fall. The boy hugged his mother the farmer, and they decided this was where they wanted to stay.

And the biggest champion of all was their new friend Fixey: Fixey the Fire Fox. "Fixey! Fixey! Fixey!" they shouted. *Snap, snap, snap!* Fixey smiled at the fairies snapping their fingers.

If you come to visit the Botanic Gardens, maybe you will be lucky and find a turtle, lions, fairies, cattle, a horse, the bats, butterflies, hawks, or crows, and maybe even a friendly fox named Fixey. If you do not find him, just try snapping your fingers, and maybe he will find you.

About the Author

JeffrAy N. Kessler is a retired schoolteacher. His inspirations come from his former students and the quirky happenings in northwest lower Michigan. *Fixey Fox Lights the Night* is his sixth book. The others are: *Colantha: A World Champion Cow; Victor the Friendly Vampire; Victor and the Bullies; Victor Finds His Family;* and *Victor Becomes a Spy.*

Printed in the USA
CPSIA information can be obtained
at www.ICGtesting.com
LVHW061201161023
761064LV00001B/2